MW01205043

TINY PAWS

Holly Chapples

Tiny Paws

ISBN-13: 978-1497372382

ISBN-10: 1497372380

Original cover art by Alicia Hope
http://www.aliciahopeauthor.blogspot.com

ACKNOWLEDGEMENTS

I wish to extend my heartfelt thanks to everyone who's helped with this book, both in the writing and in caring for the kittens who are the subjects of this book. I don't have room to list all the names, but I'd like to acknowledge just a few:

Bill Burk who convinced me to write this book.

Dan Cruzan who assisted with the stories' wording, phrasing and grammar.

Buddy Soles who provided major support for me and for the kittens.

Every volunteer at Tiny Paws for their love and dedication to all our babies.

Sally Berneathy, editor, donator and angel.

All the precious kittens that made this book possible.

THE LITTLE GIRL

The boxer chased the kitten into the little girl's yard. The dog was barking and lunging at the terrified kitten who had run behind a bush. The little girl, equally terrified by the barking, snapping dog with big jaws and sharp teeth, got between them and started shouting for help while swinging her arms at the dog.

The previous day that same boxer had caught and severely injured a kitten who had to be put out of its suffering by a neighborhood man. The little girl had seen the man stomping the head of the suffering kitten and was determined that would not happen again. Though she was frightened every minute that the dog was going to bite her, she refused to back down.

The boxer finally gave up and the girl chased him down the street, back to his owners and the fenced yard he'd escaped from.

The kitten was gone when she returned but it had been given another chance at life.

I was 8 years old and consider that my first kitten rescue.

Tiny Paws

MAGGIE

The couple was pulled over and arrested by local law enforcement. Upon searching their vehicle, the police found a mother cat and five kittens stuffed into a small plastic carrier. The kittens were about two weeks old.

As they have in the past, animal control contacted Tiny Paws to see if we could help. I picked up the momma cat and babies and took them directly to Western Veterinary Hospital. The kittens were examined, cleaned and treated for parasites. Momma cat, weak from lack of food and water and from constantly nursing five hungry little babies, was in serious condition. She had nothing left to give. The vet administered fluids and treated her for parasites then released them all to my care that evening.

At the rescue site, I put them in a small room, the kittens separate so momma could begin her healing. The kittens had a soft bed where they could snuggle down together and momma cat had a comfortable bed on a counter too high for the kittens to reach. She went right to her bed after eating, curled up and looked at me as if to say, "I'll be better soon if you can just care for my babies till then."

For the next four days, she ate and slept, never once checking on her babies. I bottle-fed the kittens and they were looking better every day. On the fifth day momma cat came down, rubbed my legs and began nursing and cleaning her babies. She was once again in charge.

Momma cat eventually weaned her kittens, and we had her and all the babies vaccinated, tested and spayed/neutered. All were ready for adoption.

A husband and wife came over to see the kittens, hopefully to adopt one for Marty, their neutered male cat who needed a playmate. While they were watching the kittens play, momma cat decided she should be the one they chose. She began rubbing the man's legs, purring and reaching up gently to paw his hands. The man petted her absently, still watching the kittens. Momma cat tried harder, purring louder and swatting at his hands until he looked down and noticed her. Maybe it was love at first sight. Maybe it was just the way it was supposed to be.

That was eight years ago. They named her Maggie and she is still a part of their family. Marty even shares his favorite sleeping spot with her. Maggie is where she belongs. She slowly closes her eyes as Marty gently grooms her.

Holly Chapples

OLGA

Olga had four three day old kittens when we rescued her. She was thin but a beautiful Russian Blue. She was friendly and made herself right at home when we offered her and her kittens a big comfy bed. Olga was a wonderful momma cat, very nurturing and attentive to her babies.

A few days after they had settled in, we received a call from a boat manufacturer in town that needed our help. While they were preparing a very large boat for transport, they found two kittens inside the boat. The kittens had to be removed from the boat so they brought them to Tiny Paws—two tiny white newborns.

We could have bottle-fed them but we thought we'd give Olga a try first.

We gently rubbed her own babies with a wash cloth then wrapped one of the new kittens in the cloth and placed it by Olga. She smelled the baby, pulled it closer and began licking the kitten. Soon both new babies were nursing and Olga was now the proud mother of not four kittens but six!

After all the kittens were weaned, we offered Olga a second orphaned litter but she decided her mothering days were behind her. She was spayed and put up for adoption.

A young man came to adopt a kitten but after hearing Olga had been our surrogate mom, he was touched by her kindness and took her home.

When we made our follow-up call, the new owner said Olga was wonderful and very talkative, which he enjoyed. After all, she had a lot to talk about and maybe was doing a little bragging about all the good things she had done.

THE SAINTS

The Saints came to us in 2012. We didn't know they were Saints then. They were just two kittens in dire need of help. I heard a knock on my door around nine in the evening. It was two women I knew. They were both frantic, both speaking over each other, both trying to convey the seriousness of the issue. None of it was easy to hear but when you run a kitten rescue, you hear a lot of things that aren't pleasant.

They handed me two kittens that were the only survivors of a tom cat attack at their farm. The two newborns were in bad shape. The little boy's stomach had been ripped open above and below his umbilical cord. The girl's back leg had been chewed down to a tiny stump with some of the bone protruding. One of the women kept asking if the kittens would be okay. I tried to be optimistic but I knew it was bad.

They needed emergency care. I contacted Dr. Fussell and we met at his vet hospital. The boy was in better shape than the girl. The vet cleaned and sutured him, and it looked like he might be okay with a little luck and a lot of love. The girl was a different story. Normally the limb would be amputated, but in this case that was not possible. She was too young for anesthesia. He decided to clean and wrap the stump and treat the kitten with antibiotics. The biggest danger was that the bone would become infected.

I took them home and began a long but amazing road of recovery and bonding.

We name all the kittens that come into the rescue. Sometimes adopting parents keep the name, sometimes they choose to change it. Watching those two kittens playing happily in spite of what they had been through, we began to think of them as little saints. St. Luke for the boy, the patron saint of children. St. Margaret for the girl, the patron saint of healing.

It was easy to see that St. Luke was very protective of his sister. He rarely left her side as she began her healing process. He cleaned her, slept by her and when she was ready to play, he was very gentle with her. Margaret was learning how to get around on three legs and was as feisty as any other kitten. She could even give her brother a good swat on occasion. She was doing well but the time had come for the next step in her healing process. She still had to have that leg removed.

The day of the surgery arrived. Luke was not happy when his sister was taken from him. He knew something was wrong and though we gave him extra attention, he could not be soothed. When Margaret came home the next day, he did not leave her side.

Tiny Paws

Margaret did great, recovering quickly and getting back to being a playful kitten. Now we just had to find them a home, together. We couldn't separate them.

A woman and her daughter came in one day and were excited to meet the pair. The daughter had a medical condition that confined her to a wheelchair. I set the two kittens on her lap and it was an instant comedy act. We all laughed as they climbed all over her and her chair. And that was that. St. Luke and St. Margaret had found their new home.

It's been over a year and the two of them are doing great. They have a home and people who love them. And while their new owners did choose to give them different names, they'll always be Luke and Margaret to us, our little saints.

FUZZ

We received a call from Animal Welfare asking us to take four 3-week old kittens that came in with their mother who had died.

The skinny young cat had shown up last winter at a city maintenance building and one of the employees began feeding her. She was very friendly and met him at the door every day for food and attention. He liked the young cat, made her a box to sleep in and called her Fuzz. By early spring she began putting on extra weight and the man soon realized she was pregnant.

A few days later, Fuzz didn't greet him at the door but instead was in her box nursing four tiny kittens. She was proud of her newborns and didn't mind when her friend held them. In the following weeks she tenderly cared for her babies and he tenderly cared for her. The kittens began to play while Fuzz and her friend both watched with joy.

Fuzz's friend was going to be gone from work for two days and ask a co-worker to feed Fuzz and watch over her kittens. The next morning the co-worker found Fuzz beside her box drooling and shaking. She fell to the floor with convulsions and in a moment was dead. With a heavy heart, he put her in the box with her kittens and took them to animal welfare.

Tiny Paws

We took the four scared orphans to our rescue where they received a lot of attention and love from our many volunteers. We got to know their personalities and named them accordingly. Eggnog was the playful one, Estelle was the quiet one, Caruso was the daring one and Yum-Yum was the eater.

We gave them their first vet exams and vaccinations at six weeks and were thrilled to learn they were healthy, active kittens. We did a newspaper article to tell the community their story and that they would be available for adoption soon.

Then one morning the nightmare began. Caruso was very sick and when Dr. Fussell examined him he told us the kitten had FIP (feline infectious peritonitis) and needed to be euthanized. Our hearts were broken but we agreed, not wanting the kitten to suffer any longer.

The little kitten's death explained what happened to Fuzz. Since FIP can be passed from momma to kittens in the womb or by nursing we knew she had probably died from this deadly disease and passed it to Caruso. There was nothing left to do for the remaining kittens but love them and wait to see what would happen.

Each one was euthanized as the symptoms became apparent and within a week all of Fuzz's beautiful kittens were gone. We were devastated. I sat in their small room, once filled with play and innocence, now filled only with sadness.

I share this story to emphasize the importance of spaying and neutering. If Fuzz had been spayed the disease would have died with her instead of her kittens. Yes, we were blessed with their short lives but it is not fair to be born just to die.

We spay and neuter all our kittens before they are adopted. In honor of Fuzz and all her babies, please spay and neuter your pets.

Tiny Paws

THE LITTLE CALICO

The four month old kitten was lying in a church parking lot, unable to walk, when a man on his way to church found her. I met him at the vet hospital and took the little calico out of his gentle hands. He looked very concerned and said he would check on her the next day.

The veterinarian studied her radiographs, looked at me and said, "This one's gonna make you mad." He pointed to two fractures in her pelvis, one on each side, and explained that those types of breaks are usually due to a stomp injury. I imagined that actually happening to the sweet little kitten and told the vet he was wrong. I wasn't mad. I was furious! Stomped and left to die. How could that happen?

The treatment didn't involve surgery since the breaks could fuse on their own with time. Strict cage confinement and rest for the next month would be her treatment. The man that found her called regularly to see how she was doing.

She looked forward each day to her cage cleaning because that's when we could hold her and love on her. She didn't complain or meow much, just took it all in stride.

On the day of re-check with the vet, the radiographs looked good and she was released from her confinement, but no jumping or climbing or playing with other kittens for another two weeks. That was a big challenge but she healed well and was released from medical care.

She was spayed and finally ready for adoption. When the new owner came to get her, I placed the little calico into the gentle hands that had saved her seven weeks before. This time we were both smiling.

ELVIRA

April 2006—January 2007

Elvira came to us through a friend who had a dog rescue. She was only a small kitten when my friend brought her to us.

From the beginning we could tell that something was wrong. We knew it, and she did too, but we didn't identify what it was until she was old enough to be litter box trained.

She was born with a neurological condition that made it impossible for her to control her bowel or her urination. There was nothing any medicine or veterinarian could do for her. Nothing short of a miracle could help.

She graciously accepted everything we could do to comfort her and seemed to understand that we couldn't make her better. She was a beautiful tortoise shell that had a spirit which often comforted **us** even as we were trying to deal with her reality.

She loved to sit in the sun to "soak up life." We had to clean and medicate her often but she was ok with it all because she knew we were trying to help.

She was happy every moment life gave her and she gave us so much joy in return. I believe she was sent to us so we would understand that, harsh as her problem was, it was part of life and was okay because she'd found people who truly cared for her.

Tiny Paws

She was only eight months old when she became so ill, we had to have her euthanized. Her ashes are in a lovely sunny spot in the rescue area but I carry with me everywhere the gift of acceptance she left me.

LOTUS AND BLOSSOM

Lotus and Blossom were sisters that came into the shelter when they were just eight weeks old. Blossom was doing well but Lotus had eye and upper respiratory infections from the feline herpes virus. She did not respond to the medications and her right eye swelled to the size of a walnut. The veterinary had to remove that eye and noted that there was infection in much of her head and remaining eye. He was correct in saying she might also be deaf.

I took Lotus home to recover from surgery. She was almost blind in the remaining eye, deaf and still on medications for infection. I put her in a room with food, water and comforts but she hardly moved or ate for days. She was depressed, getting weaker and seemed to have given up. Finally I made the decision that if she wasn't better tomorrow I would take her to the vet to end her misery.

The next morning I was awakened by a tapping sound coming from her bedroom. When I opened the door Lotus walked out and started investigating the house and the other cats. She had eaten all her food and acted like a cat with not only a will to live but a cat that had decided life would be what she made of it. As the days went by, I was totally amazed with her attitude and knew she would be happy here so I adopted her.

Two weeks later a couple came to the shelter and fell in love with Blossom. They adopted her and I'm sure she gives them as much happiness as Lotus gives me.

Lotus has been my inspiration when I'm down (rescue work can do that) and has taught me to enjoy the moment. She doesn't let anything, including her disabilities, set limits. She does whatever she wants and always seems quite proud of herself. She will soon be twelve years old and I'm sure she can live to be twenty-two if she chooses! I hope she does. I still have a lot to learn from her.

Holly Chapples

BABY LOWES

A local garden center called Tiny Paws to report a pregnant cat had climbed up to the rafters in their garden center and delivered kittens. No one knew she was there until some employees witnessed something horrible, the kittens and their mother falling from those rafters to the hard concrete below. Only one kitten survived. The momma cat's body cushioned her fall.

Still horrified about what happened, they brought the kitten to us just hours after she was born.

After examining the kitten, Dr. Fussell determined she was not injured, so our nurturing began on "Baby Lowes."

Caring for neonatal kittens is tough, especially one that young. They are very fragile. They cannot produce their own body heat so they must be kept warm. They have to be fed every two hours around the clock. They have to be kept clean. And they need prayers because a person can do all of the above, do it without fail, and neonatal kittens can still easily fade.

But Baby Lowes did not fade. She grew well and never had even the most common problems that usually occur with orphaned kittens born from feral cats. It wasn't long before this little girl won over our hearts and became our ambassador of love. When it was time to find her a home, we knew it had to be with someone as special as she was.

We posted her story and had several applicants. One couple that came to meet her took her picture with the husband's cell phone. He set Baby Lowes' picture as his wallpaper in honor of her remarkable life. Baby Lowes had found the perfect home! The wife called the day after adopting her to tell us her husband was showing her picture to co-workers as his newly adopted child.

We always do follow-up calls with our adopted kittens and when we did hers, we were told that she sits in the husband's lap every chance she gets, knowing she is safe, knowing she is loved.

PERFECT MATCH

One day Animal Welfare brought us three tiny kittens, so small they didn't even have their eyes open. We bottle fed them, and all three survived.

As they grew and began to play, we noticed one was more adventuresome and daring than the others. We named him Tough Guy because he was quite the little dare devil. However, as time passed, he began to rest more and play less, just the opposite of his siblings.

The veterinarian explained that Tough Guy had a heart murmur and would require medicine the rest of his life. That was the good news. He also told us that Tough Guy would have a short life because the heart murmur would get worse and eventually take his life. But he felt like Tough Guy was not suffering so we could take him home, give him medicine every day and try to keep him calm.

We set up a nice crate to keep him from overexerting, gave him much love and, of course, his daily medicine.

His siblings were soon adopted, but we were not sure we'd ever find a home for Tough Guy. Caring for a special needs cat such as him is a lot to ask of a potential adopter.

But sometimes fate intervenes and takes care of things. An elderly woman came to our rescue, looking for a companion. She wanted an older cat for the simple reason that she didn't want the cat to outlive her. She was worried what would happen to her pet if that happened. I was explaining that Tiny Paws always takes back our cats if needed when she spotted the crate with our little Tough Guy inside. She asked why he was confined, and we told her about his condition. All she said was, "Perfect!" She then told me that she was also on heart medication and that the two of them could just sit around, be lazy and make each other happy.

They read together. They watched TV together. They slept together. They had four months together and then Tough Guy passed away.

There are two ways to look at Tough Guy's story. It's sad that he had a short life, yes. But he was loved and gave love in that time. Can we really ask for more?

Tiny Paws

CAT FRIENDLY

When our kittens are adopted to a family that already has pets, we explain how to safely introduce them to each other and we give them a step by step information sheet to take home. We have found that this process helps reduce stress all around: on the kitten, on the new owners, and on the dogs and cats already living in the home. It seems to work pretty well. If one follows the suggestions, that is.

One adopter had taken her new kitten home, holding her against her chest as she opened the back door to let in her two labs who were "cat friendly." It went downhill pretty fast.

The two large dogs came running to see what Momma was holding. All the kitten saw was two dogs coming fast, so she reacted fast by climbing up the woman's face and jumping off her head. The scared kitten ran out the still open back door, fell into the swimming pool, climbed out and ran into an electric fence! All of this in a matter of seconds!

The adoptive mom had to go to the emergency room for facial sutures and our sweet little kitten was returned to me, traumatized.

Dr. Fussell found no obvious injuries but he was concerned about the shock she took from the electric fence. He said to take her home, observe her for lethargy, lack of appetite, vomiting or unusual behavior.

During the next few days, she seemed to be ok physically and ate normally but wasn't interested in playing with her toys or us, activities she'd formerly enjoyed.

We decided to just give her lots of affection and some more time to recover from her horrible experience.

We offered her different toys and found that she just couldn't resist dangle toys. She also discovered a little stuffed mouse that soon became her favorite toy. She was remembering how to be a kitten! Soon enough, she was back to her sweet, playful self and ready to find a new home. But I wasn't quite as ready. She had been back with us two months before I could think about letting her go and I had to be absolutely sure that she would never have to experience fear like that again.

We found her a wonderful quiet home without dogs and called several times to check on her. She was safe and a happy inside kitten.

I like to tell this story now with each adoption. I think it's more effective than a piece of paper. With a little common sense and learning from others' mistakes, new owners can experience a long and happy relationship with their kitten and hopefully prevent horrible incidents like this from ever happening again.

GRIZ

It began when a young woman in a nearby town found a tiny black kitten in her yard. The kitten was alone with no signs of a mama cat or siblings. He seemed to have something wrong with his eyes so she made an appointment with her vet. The vet gave her some antibiotic ointment and instructed her to put some in his eyes three times a day.

She realized she wasn't going to be able to keep the little guy so she called us, hoping we would take him. I agreed and she brought him over that evening. When I looked at the kitten I was shocked! His eyes were not developed and I was sure the kitten was blind. She said the vet didn't mention that, handed me the medication and left.

I stood there after she left, confused, holding a kitten that obviously needed medical attention and trying to figure out how this all happened.

After a thorough examination, Dr. Fussell said the kitten was blind, possibly due to feline herpes virus. Other than that, he said he seemed healthy. I took the kitten home and put him in a cage with another kitten his size. He was full of energy and began playing with the other kitten right away.

He was black and looked like a miniature grizzly bear so I named him Griz.

Tiny Paws

Dee, a woman who visited the rescue several times in search of a kitten for a friend, was getting to know a lot of the little furry kids, including Griz. She was amazed at how attuned he was to his environment, running around and playing with all the sighted kittens. I told her he would need a special home to accommodate his need, and she agreed he would require a lot of care.

Dee had been at the rescue a number of times when one day she noticed that Griz was in a crate by himself and was not really responding to what was going on around him. She asked what was wrong. I told her that he was quarantined due to ringworm and was lonely. She called her husband and told him she'd like to foster Griz just till he got well and could go back and run and play with the other kittens again.

That was 7 years ago. They took him home and never again thought of returning him.

They changed his name to "Beaucoup" (French for "plenty") because, as Dee puts it, "from the moment we got him he has showered us with his special gifts of knowing and being."

A friend of Dee's who is an occupational therapist helped fine tune their home so Beaucoup could get around better and taught them how to communicate with him in his non-sighted world. Dee feels it was all really easy. "We just accentuated the other senses—texture, sound, smell. I can't imagine why I ever thought it would be hard. In no time Beaucoup was making his way through our house and into our hearts. We quickly learned that he was not limited at all. We were. And as we learned more about his world, our world became even more blessed."

Last year they adopted another blind kitten from Tiny Paws, Alouette. She and Beaucoup are best buds. "They share their own special language as they play and chase each other around the house! So much fun. And such a joy to watch them live very happy, contented lives as they teach us about life itself. Special needs kitties? Their only special need is to be loved. We feel very blessed."

I saw a video of Beaucoup stalking and catching a bug in flight. He heard the bug approaching, and his head followed its path. Then, just as a sighted cat would do, he leaped up and knocked the bug out of the air and onto the ground where he captured it. I was amazed!

Beaucoup has a job now too. He is a therapy cat. Dee has a counseling business in her home and many of her patients ask for Beaucoup to join them during their session. He loves the attention and the patients love his company.

Dee said, "Not long ago my husband asked me if I thought we would ever have another sighted cat. We looked at each other and smiled. Nope. We wouldn't miss this for anything."

Tiny Paws

PATTI

My sister, Jan, my best friend and confidant, died on St. Patrick's Day. Three months later I was still grieving her.

I left my house one morning to buy supplies for the rescue shelter. I opened the door to my truck, but before I could get in, I heard a faint noise in the bushes and went to check it out. A thin, unkempt cat huddled there, lost and scared and calling out for someone to help her. I picked her up and discovered she had a collar and rabies tag.

I immediately called the vet's office listed on the tag and gave them the rabies tag number. The receptionist looked up the number in her computer and said that the cat had been missing over a month, and the owners had been looking for her all that time. I was overjoyed to hear those words.

The receptionist went on to tell me that the owners were extremely distraught about the evening they lost her. The husband backed their SUV out of their garage, not realizing the cat was on top of it. She held on and rode for a mile before she flew off the vehicle into a field. In his side mirror, the husband caught a glimpse of something flying off the top of the vehicle. Impossible as it sounded, the object looked like a cat. He made an immediate U-turn and looked for the animal but didn't find her.

Tiny Paws

When he got home their cat was missing and he knew it had been her he had seen in his mirror. The family was devastated and continued to look for their lost cat but to no avail—until the afternoon I called.

The wife answered the phone. When I told her I had found their cat, she started crying and telling her husband and children what I had said. I could hear several voices talking all at the same time. Finally the wife asked for my address and said they would be right over. I only lived about a mile and a half from them so they were at my house in no time.

When they saw their cat they all began laughing and talking excitedly. The cat meowed very softly as I handed her to them. She settled into their arms, obviously happy to be back with her family.

They thanked me for finding her and said they loved her very much. I could tell that! The wife told me the cat's name was Patti because she was born on St Patrick Day.

I blurted out, "She's my sister!" I was as shocked to hear those words come from my mouth as the woman was. I explained that my sister had died on St. Pat's Day and since that time I had felt very lost and alone, just like little Patti. The woman smiled, took her cat and quickly left.

I'm certain the family was thankful to get their beloved cat back. I'm also certain they thought I was a nut case.

Getting Patti back to her loving home helped me know that Jan would want me to be ok, just like Patti. It was like two reunions with happy endings that day.

Now every St Patrick's Day, I celebrate Jan's life. I always think about Patti also, the lost cat I rescued who likewise rescued me.

SIAMESE IF YOU PLEASE!

On July 10, 2011, an urgent call interrupted my otherwise semi-normal afternoon at the rescue. A cat breeder asked if we would take a momma Siamese and her three one-week old, nursing babies. She had previously sold some of her registered cats and taken others to Animal Welfare. These four were all that were left. The woman was from California, hated the Oklahoma heat, and was, therefore, driving back to California the next morning. She wasn't taking them with her.

We hurried over only to find a double-wide mobile home in the middle of a pasture in 115 dry Oklahoma degrees. It was five in the afternoon, still in the heat of the day. I remember the sight upon entering the home. Momma cat and her kittens were in a corner, panting and lethargic from the extreme heat. We gently placed them in a carrier and immediately transferred them to our air conditioned vehicle, which we had chilled down.

Arriving at our foster home, we put them in a cool room with food, water, litter, bedding and toys. Momma and all three babies were in terrible condition. They were thin, had eye infections and diarrhea, and, of course, heat exhaustion. The veterinarian came to the house for exams instead of transporting them so as not to traumatize them any more.

After weeks of care and treatment, they began to get healthy and strong. Momma cat played with her babies, running and hiding and chasing.

Momma cat was a registered classic Siamese. Dad was Burmese (so the registration stated). This momma cat had just birthed a previous litter in late March. She had been a baby factory!

We still don't know how any survived the conditions in that tin oven with no air-conditioning. The real hero is Momma. We are still in awe when we think of what a good momma she was despite nearly dying.

Our foster mom named the babies Hickory, Dickory and Doc. The kittens were gorgeous! All were spayed and neutered (no more litters for momma cat) and placed up for adoption.

Momma cat got adopted by a wonderful couple that immediately fell in love with her. One kitten was taken by a college student, another went to a vet student, and the last kitten was adopted by a retired lady. All of them are loved and spoiled!

Tiny Paws

THE BRICK WALL

One evening a young girl was walking down an alley when she saw some teenage boys toss something against a brick wall. They tossed it, retrieved it and drew back to toss it again.

The neighborhood wasn't the best, there were several boys in the group, all bigger and older than her, and she was alone. Hoping to avoid trouble, the girl started to walk on, but something made her look more closely at the object the boy clutched. It wasn't a rock or an old shoe or some other item of garbage. It was a kitten.

A powerful surge of anger washed over her, replacing the fear. Suddenly she couldn't walk away. She strode over and snatched the kitten from the clutches of the boy who held it. Apparently astonished at her fury, the boys stood back and said nothing.

The kitten was still alive but in bad shape. She got away from the boys as fast as possible.

She called us, very distraught, so we met her at Western Vet Hospital. She said she didn't know what happened to her, what gave her the courage to rescue the kitten, that she just became so angry at what they were doing that the anger overcame any fear. She knew she had to save that kitten.

Luckily the kitten did not have any broken bones or internal injuries. He did have a few scrapes and bruises and was traumatized.

At the rescue building we put him in a cage and placed a small cardboard box in his cage. He hid in that box for the first week. With much patience, affection and yummy threats he gradually became less fearful. By the third week he would leap into our arms when we opened his cage. He trusted humans again in spite of his cruel experience.

The young girl that saved the kitten came to see him before he was adopted. I told her she should be proud because she saved the kitten's life. I also told her to beware because she might find herself doing that the rest of her life.

###

For anyone interested in learning more about Tiny Paws Kitten Rescue:

Website:
tinypawsok.org
Email:
tinypawsok@gmail.com
Facebook:
https://www.facebook.com/pages/Tiny-Paws-Kitten-Rescue/164254803592526
Twitter:
@_tinypaws.

Made in the USA
San Bernardino, CA
25 March 2014